Awesome DESIGN

25 THINGS

YOU SHOULD KNOW BEFORE BECOMING A GRAPHIC DESIGNER

SECOND EDITION

SECOND EDITION
Shannel Wheeler, Author, Illustrator and Designer
Cover Design by Shannel Wheeler
Deanna Hart, Editor

www.makeawesomedesign.com

Dedication

Many thanks to those who have inspired me to write this book. To God, for being my supreme inspiration; To a very special person and my awesome business partner, Eric, for always encouraging me, supporting me and pushing me towards my full potential; To my original design partner in crime, Halle Malcomb, with whom I first ventured down the road of entrepreneurship; To my college design professor, R. Brian Stone, who taught me many invaluable lessons about good design and who led by example; and to author extraordinaire, Nadia Mathews, for planting that extra seed to help me get started on this book. A special thanks to my loving parents who have always supported me in everything I've done, and who have nurtured my artistic abilities and tolerated my crazy "only child" projects. To my closest friends, to all of my cool designer friends, to my inspiring entrepreneur friends, to my extended family, and to those who have inspired me to step out of my comfort zone and reach for my dreams — thank you!

....

Special thanks to Deanna Hart. You rock!

So, who is this book for anyway?

Are you thinking about becoming a graphic designer? Not sure if it's the right career choice for you? Are you totally clueless to what graphic design is? Or, are you just getting started on your graphic design journey? If your answer is "yes" to any of those questions, then this book is for you! This book is not for experienced designers, senior designers or "design ninjas" — they already know all or most of this stuff. I've written this especially for newbies, like you, who want an overview of what it takes to be a graphic designer and what to expect in a graphic design career.

Inside, you will receive a basic design overview, an understanding of what's involved in pursuing this career, and what you need to become successful at it. We'll tackle questions, fundamentals, myths, truths, and a few extra topics that will hopefully help you figure out if graphic design is for you. And just for fun, I'll even add in a few of my own personal stories to show you that everything I'm talking about — I went through myself!

By the end of this book, I hope you'll have a deeper understanding about graphic design — and maybe you'll join the club, too! I hope to inform, enlighten, excite and inspire you to take that first step to becoming the designer you want to be.

?

5

QUESTIONS

What do graphic designers do?
Can they make money? Get answers to some
of your basic, need-to-know questions!

1. Why should you care about graphic design?

Before we answer this question, let's use our imagination for a minute. Picture these scenarios in your mind:

- Walking through an airport without any signs telling you where to go
- A major retailer that doesn't sell name brand clothing
- Entering a fast food restaurant without any exterior signs, photos, colors or advertisements
- Working for a big company that doesn't have a logo or brand
- Shopping in a toy store where all the aisles are filled with only plain cardboard boxes and no actual toys on display
- Going to a bookstore where every last book looks exactly the same — photo-less, white paperbacks with only the title and author name stamped in small print on the spine

Sounds kind of weird, right? But, really. Just imagine it. Graphic design is more important than you might think. In fact, for centuries, design — from printmaking in the 1500s to today's ever-evolving digital age — has shaped and influenced human life. And, that's pretty cool. Design guides, shapes, influences, persuades, informs, educates and entertains us. It's the bridge between an idea or message and the visual form that it takes on in the world. I bet that at least half of what you touch, see, consume or buy has graphic design applied to it in some way.

Without graphic design, not only would our world be pretty boring, but we would be left without a lot of important — and necessary — information. We also would have a hard time distinguishing between products and services, and there would be a lack of identity across everyday objects.

A WORLD WITHOUT GRAPHIC DESIGN

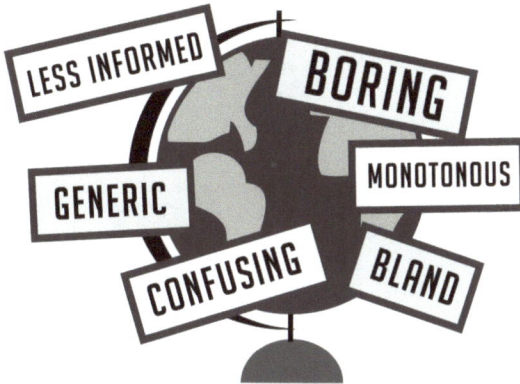

Graphic design uses images, text, color, and other creative elements to solve problems visually. Design shapes the everyday things in our lives — from the small things that we might not even notice (say a label on a water bottle) to the big things that bombard us (that commercial you've already seen five times today) — and gives them visual meaning.

There has been — and still remains — a long-standing need for visual cues that connect people to a message. Because of that, our world will always need design — and good design at that. And, that's great news for us designers.

2. How does a graphic designer become a hero?

OK, so the world has a lot of visual problems that need to be solved. What can you do about it? Who can you help? Graphic designers always ask the question, "What's the best way that I can visualize a solution to a problem in a way that will be effective to the people who will see it?"

HOW DOES A GRAPHIC DESIGNER BECOME A HERO?

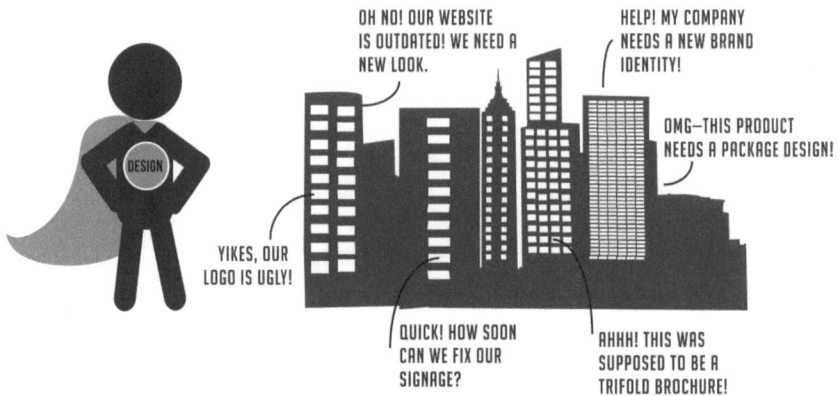

OH NO! OUR WEBSITE IS OUTDATED! WE NEED A NEW LOOK.

HELP! MY COMPANY NEEDS A NEW BRAND IDENTITY!

OMG—THIS PRODUCT NEEDS A PACKAGE DESIGN!

YIKES, OUR LOGO IS UGLY!

QUICK! HOW SOON CAN WE FIX OUR SIGNAGE?

AHHH! THIS WAS SUPPOSED TO BE A TRIFOLD BROCHURE!

Graphic designers save the day by using their creative super powers. Well, kind of. Really, there's more to it than that. Graphic designers use lots of technical skill, a healthy dose of analytical thinking, plenty of observational skills, a bit of intuition, and loads of creativity to produce meaningful work. They use a combination of images, graphics, text and color to create visual solutions.

Not only do good designers know how to create something that looks good, but they know how to come up with a solution that effectively communicates a message to the people who need to see it.

Graphic designers use their brainpower and other essential tools such as computer software (and yes, even a good ole' pencil and paper) to execute their ideas. When given a task, they gather all the background information necessary, using that information to come up with a printed or digital design solution. In addition, graphic designers often incorporate other niche elements or specialties into their work, such as illustration, photography, animation or computer programming.

DESIGN SAVES THE DAY

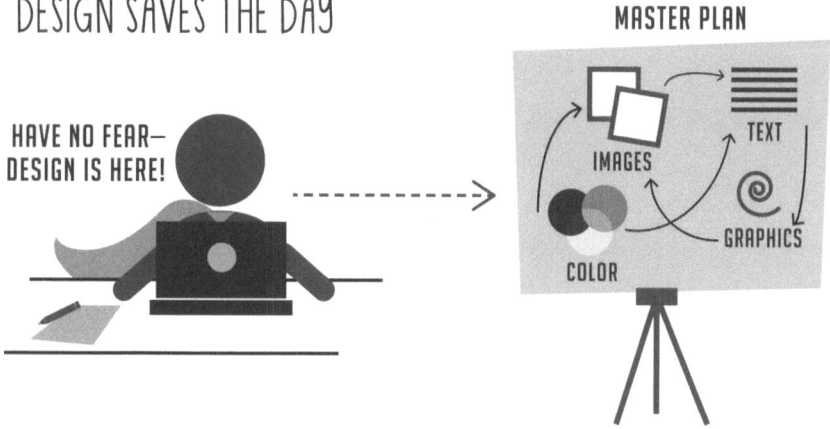

MASTER PLAN

HAVE NO FEAR—
DESIGN IS HERE!

IMAGES

TEXT

COLOR

GRAPHICS

Because the industry is so broad, as an emerging graphic designer, you can explore many different avenues. Maybe you will discover that you like creating brands or corporate identities. Perhaps, you will work primarily with print design like publications or signage. Or, maybe your focus will be websites, mobile platforms, or even programming. You can even design for retail markets or design packaging for various products.

Graphic designers can work for corporations, small businesses, agencies, design firms or non-profits. Or, they can decide to work for themselves. Graphic designers can work across all types of industries and for all types of people. There is no "box" or one area that graphic designers must work in. The opportunities are endless!

SPECIALTIES CAN STEM FROM GRAPHIC DESIGN

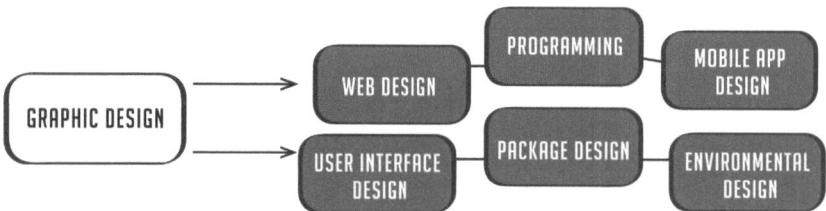

GRAPHIC DESIGN

WEB DESIGN

PROGRAMMING

MOBILE APP DESIGN

USER INTERFACE DESIGN

PACKAGE DESIGN

ENVIRONMENTAL DESIGN

3. So, is it rocket science?

Anything worth doing will have its challenges along the way. And, as I have learned throughout my own career, graphic design is no different. Whether you are naturally gifted or just learning the basics, there will be some learning curves, some rough patches, and some points of frustration. That's just a normal — and inevitable — part of the process. Just go with it! There are so many amazing things you will learn along the way.

Graphic designers not only have to think creatively but critically, as well. When generating ideas, you will need to first gather information. Then, plan out your strategy, get creative by using the skill of your hands through drawing/sketching and/or using design software, and then deliver the final product. In addition, you'll need to learn how to clearly communicate your ideas, take direction well, and be a thought leader.

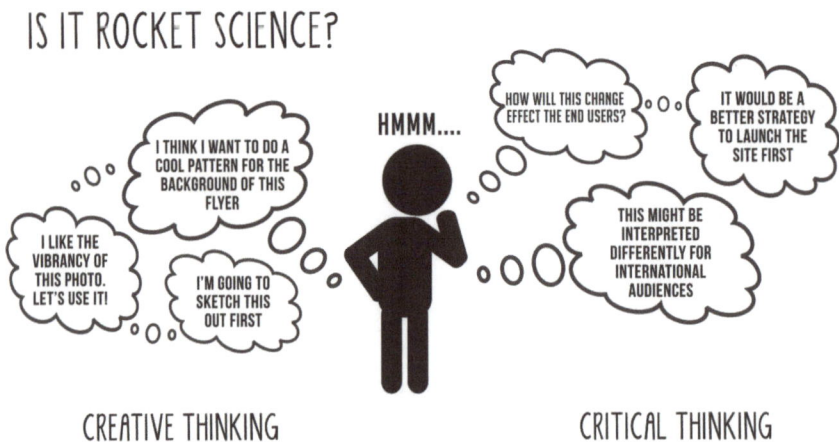

IS IT ROCKET SCIENCE?

I THINK I WANT TO DO A COOL PATTERN FOR THE BACKGROUND OF THIS FLYER

HMMM....

HOW WILL THIS CHANGE EFFECT THE END USERS?

IT WOULD BE A BETTER STRATEGY TO LAUNCH THE SITE FIRST

I LIKE THE VIBRANCY OF THIS PHOTO. LET'S USE IT!

I'M GOING TO SKETCH THIS OUT FIRST

THIS MIGHT BE INTERPRETED DIFFERENTLY FOR INTERNATIONAL AUDIENCES

CREATIVE THINKING

CRITICAL THINKING

Is it rocket science? No. But it does require you to think! Despite the challenges, graphic design can be extremely fulfilling if you pursue it with passion and determination. Being "hard" is a matter of perspective, but the fulfillment that you will receive from creating something that is meaningful, influential and potentially life-changing will trump all the discomforts.

4. Can you make money?

Well, of course! How much money you make though is determined by how far you want to go. It's as simple as that. According to creative staffing agency, *The Creative Group's 2014 Salary Guide*[1] (figures vary by geographic location, industry, job requirements, and of course, by skill level and experience), an entry-level graphic designer can earn an average of $35K. A skilled, experienced designer with between three and five years of experience may earn an average annual salary of $55-60K each year. A senior level designer may earn $70K annually or more per year. Leadership positions such as art directors and creative directors can make an average annual salary of $100K annually or more. But as an entrepreneur, there is no salary cap to what you can earn. It all depends on the type of opportunities you pursue and how hard you are willing to work.

CAN YOU MAKE MONEY?

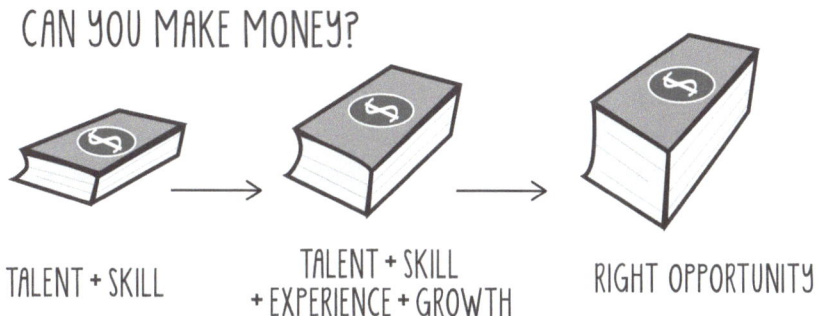

TALENT + SKILL → TALENT + SKILL + EXPERIENCE + GROWTH → RIGHT OPPORTUNITY

The great thing about graphic design is that there will always be a need for it. Those who value good design and understand its importance will be willing to pay you what it's worth.

5. Do you love it?

Let's see. Do you love being creative? Do you enjoy solving problems? Are you capable of learning computer software and using it as a primary tool? Then yes, you could be a graphic designer. You could probably even become really successful. The question is are you motivated, determined and excited about graphic design? Do you have the drive to travel down this challenging, yet rewarding, career path? If you can place a check mark next to those questions, then I believe you are ready to pursue a graphic design career!

When I was first beginning my graphic design journey, I applied to more than 100 graphic design jobs before finally landing my first full-time design gig. I racked up countless hours working until the wee hours of the morning and tolerated more than my fair share of crazy clients. Needless to say, I even developed an addiction to $4 coffee. This was my experience. But it doesn't mean that this is the path that you will take as you begin your own journey. I say this because I didn't do all of those things because I simply *like* design. I endured those experiences because I actually *love* it! I love the ability to be creative, transform thoughts into a visual reality, and build big results from small ideas. I love getting lost in my own thoughts, exploring shapes and colors, and piecing together words and images to make something meaningful.

But more than all those things, I love how I am able help people through graphic design. When someone tells me how my work has transformed or added value to his or her business, when I hear that a client wants to turn the logo I created into a tattoo, when what I have done puts a genuine smile on someone's face — that is what really drives me. I'm so grateful that I'm doing something I love.

If you aspire to become a graphic designer, I hope that you have a natural love for creating and a genuine curiosity to learn about design and its power. After all, that will take you much farther than just designing solely for the money, because someone told you it was easy, or for some other misinformed reason. Maybe, like me, you love art or maybe you discovered design through your interest in computer technology. However you discovered graphic design, I hope that you have a genuine passion for it. But, if you don't love it yet, I hope that you are beginning to fall in love with it. You will need that passion if you want to progress in this industry. My advice is to make sure that you're pursuing graphic design for the right reason — because you truly want to!

5
FUNDAMENTALS

*All great designers understand the
key fundamentals that are critical to creating
successful designs. You should know them, too!*

6. You must become a creative problem solver

When you hear the term "graphic designer", do you know what that really means? Does a graphic designer just make logos and business cards? Does graphic design involve creating websites? Is it taking plain information and turning it into something fancy?

It was a Thursday morning, and I was going in for a second interview for a senior graphic designer position at an acclaimed engineering company. The first interview had been pretty successful, considering that I didn't know much about engineering.

However, I sold my case by convincing them that I would be taking a fresh approach and designing from the perspective of their customers, who weren't necessarily experts in engineering either. Nice sell, right?

During the interview, I met with one of the managers who cut straight to the chase, explaining that they had a whole bunch of product collateral and sales sheets that all looked different and disjointed. He began spreading out numerous papers across his desk so that I could easily see each sheet. He wanted to know, if I was hired, how I would tie all these pieces together to make their collateral looked unified and recognizable. Without hesitation, he handed me a marker and said, "Okay go up to that board and draw me your solution." The first thing that came to my mind was, "Is this guy serious!?!"

So, back to my earlier question, "What does it mean to be a graphic designer?" It can — and does — involve creating logos and websites, and making something look nice. But it's a little deeper than that. As a designer, it is going to be your task to solve problems creatively. More often than not, those problems are going to include at least one of two tasks:

1) Creating a new visual solution from a thought or an idea

2) Fixing an existing visual and making it better

In other words, you'll either be creating something new or improving something that already exists.

When contemplating the manager's question during this intense interview, my mind raced a thousand miles a minute, and my palms began to sweat. But, I developed a solution: create a color-coded template system that would tie everything together but still distinguish the company's various products. Upon hearing my answer, he gave a nod of approval, and I took a huge sigh of relief. Later, I was offered the position. You may not have to solve creative problems under that type of pressure, but you should be equipped to think critically about a problem presented to you and how you can potentially solve that problem. Once you've figured out the best and most logical direction, you will need to create a tangible solution.

What other types of problems do graphic designers have to solve? Here are just a few examples:

- Create a brand identity for a new local ice cream shop
- Create directional signage for a museum exhibit
- Put together a 200-page product catalog for a national retailer
- Redesign a website for a growing community college
- Create a direct mail piece for a political campaign
- Make a series of sales sheets for an automotive company
- Design a wedding invitation
- Reformat an online newsletter for a local library
- Create visual graphics for an extensive social media campaign
- Design the CD cover for a popular music artist

Each one of the above examples requires creative problem solving. As a graphic designer, your work can have a positive impact on people, companies and organizations. You're not just making something look nice. Rather, you are actually solving a problem, fulfilling a need, and making a difference. And when you can make an impression with a recognizable, effective, positive and/or memorable design, you have executed successful, creative problem solving.

7. You need to know what makes good design

You're in a room with just a desk and a chair. You've been given the task to come up with an impressive design. What is the first thing you need to create your design? A computer? Maybe a pencil and sketchpad? A creative brief?

Before anything else, the first thing you need to know is what makes good design. Good design is something that's eye-catching, stimulating, impressive, cool, effective and influential — all those good things that help solve problems and communicate messages effectively. You can't even begin to tackle a project successfully if you don't have an understanding of good design and how to apply it to your own work. If you are a naturally creative or artistic person, you may think you've got this one in the bag. But don't be fooled. Just having great ideas doesn't always translate to good design. Simply picking a nice font, a decent image and slapping together a seemingly "cool" layout doesn't automatically mean you understand good design.

Whenever you see a design that really catches your eye — an innovative website layout, a quirky logo, or a magazine cover that blows your mind — it's not by chance! There is a strategy behind good design, and creating something memorable and effective requires a conscious effort to pull it off.

Think of an experienced chef carrying out a recipe. He knows the right ingredients to use, what utensils he needs to complete the recipe, and the skills required to successfully put all the ingredients together. Creating good design is similar. It requires knowledge, careful thought, creativity, skill, and proper execution of the ingredients. How you use the ingredients will be determined by what the recipe calls for (requirements of the design). These ingredients? Let's call them **design principles**.

RECIPE FOR SUCCESS

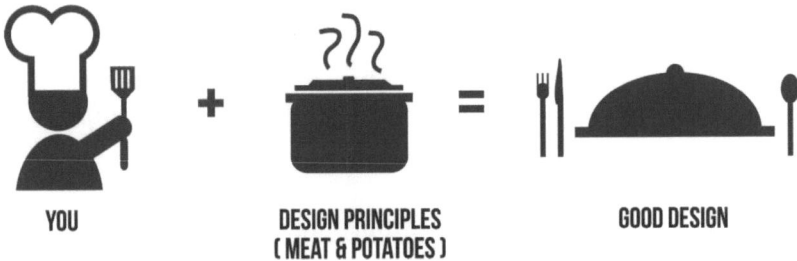

YOU + DESIGN PRINCIPLES
(MEAT & POTATOES) = GOOD DESIGN

Before we get into what some of the primary design principles are, please understand that learning them is a process. I'll provide you with a broad overview, but you will need to take the time to explore these concepts much more in depth to fully understand them. If you don't "get it" all at once, don't worry. It takes practice. Many new designers don't truly grasp how all of these principles work together at first glance. But with time, consistent practice and good examples to guide you, everything will make sense. As you design, be mindful of how you are using these principles collectively, or if you are even applying them at all.

So, let's check out the following principles, which apply to both print and digital design.

10 principles for good design:

Message (what the design means)

The message is what drives the direction of the design and dictates what the design is communicating and to whom. In essence, the message tells a story that can be communicated with words, images or both. The viewer should be able to take something away from the message of the design, whether it's information, a call to action, inspiration, or something else.

MESSAGE

WE'RE OPEN

PARTY OVER HERE

STOP

BETTER PRODUCTS
BUY NOW

FREE PIZZA

Hierarchy (determining what's most important)

Hierarchy places priority on the elements of your layout, whether they are text, images or graphics. So, now that you have a message, what's the most important part of that message? What's the second most important part, third, and so on? You can show hierarchy in various ways, including placement, size and color.

HIERARCHY

GRAND OPENING — MOST IMPORTANT

DEC 1, 2014 | NOON-4PM — IMPORTANT

1234 NEW AVE. — IMPORTANT

MEET OUR FRIENDLY STAFF! — LESS IMPORTANT

Placement/Spacing/Alignment (where you put things)
Where and how you place text and images within your layout can make or break your design. Placement focuses on the positioning of elements and making best use of the space available. Spacing deals with the proximity — how close or far away — the design elements are from each other. Alignment describes how elements line up with each other and how they line up with the overall space.

PLACEMENT / SPACING / ALIGNMENT

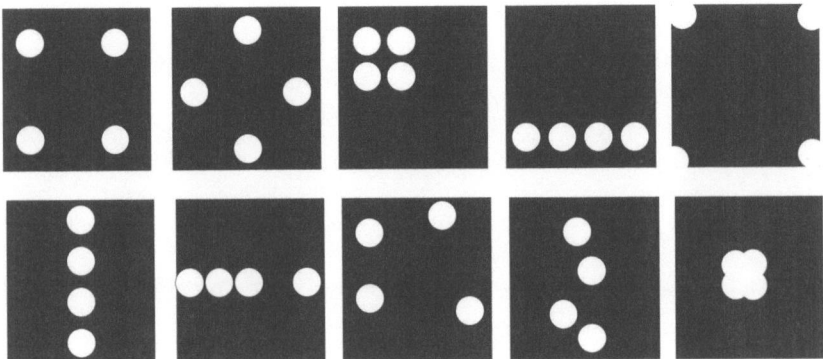

Color (well, this is self explanatory)

Color works in many ways to give life and vibrancy to your design. It can also create deeper meaning within your design. Color can be literal (i.e. a red apple) or color could symbolize greater messages (i.e. purple for royalty). Color is often dictated by many factors such as personal preference, a company's brand standards, or its relationship to the subject matter.

COLOR

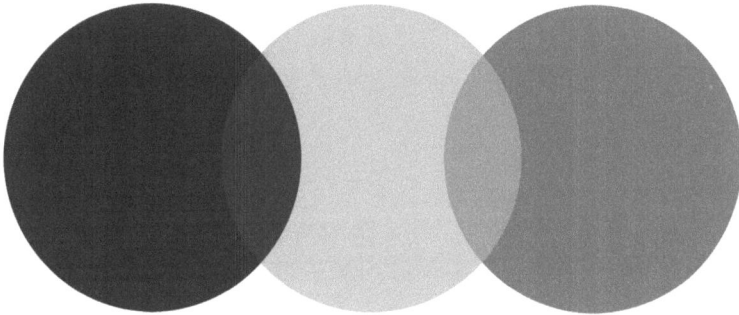

Typography (use of letterforms and fonts)

Typography describes the use of typefaces/fonts and letterforms to display content or to be used as artistic elements. The way that you organize your words/text onto the page can influence how well your audience will understand your message. That's why it's important to consider the type of font(s) you are using, as well as the size, weight (thickness), color, and placement of the type.

TYPOGRAPHY

Imagery (you know what this is too)

Imagery comes in various forms, including photographs, graphics, icons, illustrations and charts/graphs. Use imagery in a way that connects to the overall message that you must communicate.

IMAGERY

PHOTOGRAPH

GRAPHIC

ICON

Contrast (opposites attract)

Contrast is the existence of opposing elements. This can include contrast of color, size, shape, space and more. Contrast allows for emphasis in your design.

CONTRAST

SIZE   COLOR   SHAPE

Balance (just enough of "this" and "that")

Balance within your design ensures that certain elements don't ineffectively outweigh others, allowing the eye to flow easily through the layout. Balance allows focal points to be evident, but not overwhelmingly prominent.

BALANCE

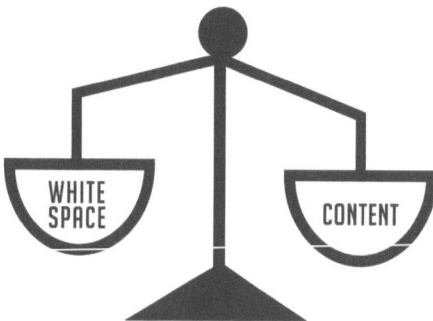

Tone (what's the attitude?)
Tone determines the feel or attitude that your design depicts. Do you want the audience to feel happy or sad when they look at your work? Does the message in your design portray positivity or negativity? Humor or empathy?

TONE

HAPPY　　SAD　　INFORMATIONAL　PROVOKING　EMPATHY

Form and Function (how it looks and how it works)
The quote "form follows function" — which was coined from architect Louis Sullivan during the 20th century Industrial Age — has been a debatable statement for years, implying that the function of the design takes precedence over the visual appeal of the design. But, it's important to have balance between what you want your design to do (its main purpose) and how you want it to look. While your designs should always strive to be visually appealing, make sure that they are satisfying the needs of the audience and effectively relaying the messages that need to be expressed.

FORM AND FUNCTION

 +

Knowing how to design well means understanding what makes good design. Design principles are the foundation of your design skill set. Understanding the principles of good design will carry you much farther than just touching the surface with cookie-cutter solutions like ready-made graphics or templates. When you understand good design, you can apply it using any software program and to any project. No matter how much technology advances, these principles never change.

8. Process is mandatory for success

Here's a scenario: If a client asked you to create a five-page brochure detailing their products and services, what is the first step you would take? What's the second step? Fourth, fifth and so on…? How would you go about starting the project, and how would you finish it? Would you approach this project the same way you would approach a logo design?

Now that you understand that good principles are necessary for good design, you also must understand the steps you need to take to successfully complete any design project. The same way a contractor wouldn't build a house without a solid process from start to finish, you should not design without a process either. There should be consistent steps you take each time you design to ensure that you are putting out your best work.

Using a good design process is actually critical to your success and growth as a graphic designer. And the longer you design, the more you'll realize this! There's definitely an advantage to dividing your projects into phases. Doing this will keep you organized and focused on important tasks. It can be pretty tempting to take shortcuts or easy routes to solve problems. But in the long run, shortcuts can stifle your overall growth and will most likely lead to poorly executed designs.

There are different processes out there, but here are the fundamental steps for creating a successful design from start to finish:

DESIGN PROCESS

| RESEARCH | PLAN / SKETCH | CREATE | REVISE / REFINE | FINALIZE |

Research

The beginning stages of a new design project should entail some type of research during which you take the time to understand what and for whom you are designing. In other words, what is this project about, and what are the objectives? Who is it for and who gives the final approval? What is the timeline to complete it? Gather any background information that may help put the project into context, and fill in as many knowledge gaps as possible so that you can fully comprehend the scope of the project.

The amount of research you do will depend on how much time you have to spend on the project, how much is at stake, and how and for whom the design will be used. Research could be as in depth as studying months of market analysis, conducting client interviews, viewing end user surveys, or reading supplemental literature. Or, research could be as simple as doing a quick Google search, making a brief phone call, or skimming through a few relevant documents. Either way, gather enough information to confidently move forward with the project.

Plan/write/sketch

It may surprise you, but there are graphic designers who skip this important step and go straight to designing. While there are situations where that may work, for the most part, you should always take the time to plan. We've all heard the saying, "If you fail to plan, you plan to fail." Well this is true, especially for design.

Planning your design will help you organize your thoughts and give you a road map to help you create your design. Before you begin, sketch out your ideas, jot down helpful key words, create a web map or draw a flow chart. By planning ahead, you will discover that it's much easier to make changes on the front end of a project (rearranging a storyboard or reworking a web page's architecture on paper) than it is to make these huge changes on the back end after spending valuable time and resources. Good planning will help prevent those types of errors and help you stay on track with your deadlines.

While you are planning, remember to keep your client (this could also be your professor or boss) aware of your plans, too. Keeping them involved in the beginning stages of the design process allows everyone to stay on track. This is also the time when critical decisions can be made, and both parties can feel confident that they are moving in the same direction. Planning is often an iterative process, so don't always expect that you will nail your idea on the first try.

Create

Now this is the fun part! This is where you actually design! You should be using the insight you gained from your research, planning and sketches to guide you in the creation of your design concept. Sometimes you may have free reign to design whatever you please, and at other times, you will have guidelines to work within. In any case, this is where you show off your skills and talents, delve into your design software, pull out all the tricks, and let your innovation shine.

Revise/refine

You didn't think you were done, did you? On a rare occasion, you might knock your design out of the park, producing a spotless piece of work. But more often than not, your design will need to be refined in some way, so do not think it strange if your client, boss or teacher isn't in total agreement with your initial approach. You may not have captured the message in the most effective way, there may be technical or grammatical errors, the client may have made changes to the content, or the scope of the entire project may have changed. Or, perhaps you just thought of a better way to solve the problem.

Revising your work is naturally the next step in fine tuning and sculpting your design into something great. It will also challenge your thought process, and most likely, your greatest ideas will not always be your first ideas. So, expect to make changes!

Finalize/Produce

Once your design satisfies all parties involved, it's time to finalize and produce it, if applicable. This is where you package and send final files, send items to print, upload an approved site to the client's server, or maybe publish your app in the marketplace. You may even need to create supporting documentation, archive files, provide training, or do a follow up, which will depend on your final product and your responsibilities.

....

At the end of the day, make sure that you are using some type of design process on a consistent basis. If you're not using any process, start now! Having one in place will inevitably save you a lot of time and headache.

9. Design. Repeat. Design. Repeat.

As I was preparing my final project during my senior year of college, I had a meeting with my professor about some logo concepts I was creating. The logos represented a re-brand of a cultural center on campus, and I showed him about five or six concepts. He asked me to explain the message behind the concepts I created, and I happily described the thought process behind my designs. But then he asked to see more. So I went back to the drawing board and created more concepts. I met with him again, and he told me my new designs were good, but I needed to explore more concepts. Okay, fine. So, I went my way again and came up with even more concepts. And again, I showed him my latest designs — complete with explanations for each one — and once again, I was asked to create more. By this point, I was highly annoyed and kind of bummed that I had not finalized a logo. Nevertheless, I presented him with another round of concepts. Again, I had to explain the logic behind the refined concepts. But the best part was that he finally gave me a nod of approval, and I was able to move on to the next phase of the project. Whew! After all of that, I had created more than 50 variations of different logos! Later, I realized that my professor was trying to teach me a lesson beyond just a logo design.

So by now I'm sure you're asking, "What's the point?" The point is that my senior project gave me a new perspective on my design process. I learned that getting a design just right may take multiple attempts, and I had to be willing to persevere and design over and over and over again to be successful.

If you want to be great at something, you have to practice — a lot. But you already knew that, didn't you? Do you have dreams of one day mastering every design program? Or are you mesmerized by the amazing design work printed in a magazine or posted online, wondering how long will it take for you get to that level? Most graphic designers want to get to a point where they can pull the cool ideas from their heads and make those ideas look just as cool on paper or on screen as they do in their minds. But truthfully, that takes skill. And, skill takes practice.

So, how do you get there? Well, work on improving your design skills daily. If you don't have a project to work on, then try completing a certain number of design tutorials each week. Try recreating that cool design that you saw recently or learning a new tool or effect in a design software program. Continually improve your techniques, and create benchmarks to evaluate your growth over time.

As you practice your design skills, don't be afraid to make mistakes. Becoming a great designer is a journey, and you need to go through the process of trial and error to grow. You must realize that there will not be a day when you wake up and say, "I have arrived!" Everyone learns differently, and sometimes it may take you a while to "get it". That's okay. Just remember that the more you design and the more you practice, the better you will become. You will begin to train your mind to think "good design".

You will be faster, more proficient, more intuitive, more savvy, and you will develop your own style, creating more opportunities for you to improve. If I were to look back today on those logos I created almost 10 years ago, I would probably laugh. But daily practice over the years has made me a much better designer today.

Above all else — including talent, natural ability and opportunity — consistent practice over time with a mindset of growth is what develops an awesome graphic designer!

10. Versatility is good

While I was in college, I worked as a part-time designer at an educational facility. I didn't know anything about pre-made vector graphics at the time, so I hand drew everything, scanned it, and traced over it in Adobe Illustrator. I also remember working as a design intern and getting my feet wet at a small law firm in Virginia where I did heavy Photoshop production, text layout and even motion graphics. After moving to Atlanta, a few years later, I received a large dose of experience while working as a graphic designer at a travel and incentive company. I also contracted at a magazine publishing company, where I worked long hours, toiled with out-of-date software and drank lots of coffee to stay awake. But, I learned a lot. Years later, I had the privilege of designing an entire magazine on my own for an up-and-coming non-profit organization. I even gained special experiences at small agencies, and I learned about big budgets and processes working at large corporations. However, the hardest but most fulfilling work I've ever done is the work that I've done for myself, designing for my own businesses and clients.

I have completed a range of projects, from small business branding and technical spec sheets to app design and wedding programs. I have collaborated within small groups and across large departments. I have met with clients in person while some were thousands of miles away, and whom I've never personally met. I've done clean, corporate design and edgy, unapologetic design. Some of it I enjoyed, and some of it I could I have lived without. But the diversity of my experience has shaped and molded my identity as a graphic designer — the designer that I am today.

As you take this journey, be sure to work on different types of projects. If you discover what you're good at early on, go for it! Just don't forget to explore what other design strengths you might have. Learn different design techniques. Experiment with different design styles. You don't have to be a jack of all design trades, but having a diverse range of experience helps you to be well rounded.

Exploring different design avenues — layout, web design, corporate design, abstract design, large format design, branding and so on — is a great way to help you discover what you like and what you don't. After all, you don't want to end up doing the same type of design over a long period of time without having explored other options. Don't get me wrong. There's nothing wrong with having a signature style or niche that makes you unique, but don't let that confine you to forever designing in only one way.

Maybe your strength is simple layouts or corporate branding, or maybe you are really strong in creating innovative, abstract pieces of work. Maybe you're really comfortable using Photoshop and haven't really given much thought to InDesign. Maybe you haven't figured out what your strengths in design are yet. In any case, keep an open mind because you might discover new aspects of design that really interest you.

5
MYTHS

What you thought you knew about graphic design may not be true! Discover and dispel some of those myths you may have heard.

11. You have to know how to draw

When I got my first full-time design job, I worked with a lot of really good designers. Some were well versed in print design, others in website design, and some excelled at both. They would create the most unique and thoughtful layouts. Sometimes I would examine their work files just to admire them or try and figure out how they did it. Some won awards for their designs and others got notoriety for their forward thinking and consistent creativity. One day, I was brainstorming with one of those great designers about a new project they were working on and the imagery they could use. The designer had been searching for a specific graphic without success, so I asked, "Why don't you just draw it?" To my surprise, she chuckled and very matter-of-factly told me that she could not draw worth a lick.

You might be surprised to know that if you want to become a graphic designer, you do not have to know how to draw. Of course, while having an artistic hand is valuable, you can still be a great designer even if drawing is not a skill you possess. You don't have to have advanced art classes under your belt or even have a remote interest in the Pietas of Michelangelo. It is not a requirement.

I grew up painting, drawing, building and creating every chance I could. I had more sketchbooks than I could count, and I was always longing to have the latest and greatest "art kit". I loved building with Legos, and I would paint or draw portraits of friends and family as birthday presents when I couldn't afford anything else. For me, painting and drawing was my bridge to graphic design, but that might not be your story.

While you may not be able to draw, you must be able to *compose* . What I mean is that even if you can hardly draw a stick figure, you need to know how to put all of the design elements together — text, images, graphics, lines and shapes — and do it successfully to create something with meaning. If this isn't a skill you already possess, then it's a skill you should begin to develop.

Don't get me wrong. Having the ability to draw has great advantages within graphic design. If you have the ability to create your own artwork, assets, illustrations or graphics, that is a powerful weapon to carry in your design arsenal. Creating something "by hand" that another designer may have to find through stock photos or vectors is a powerful advantage. Utilizing artistic abilities is a great way for designers to elevate their work and add value to their creative skill sets.

However, every situation may not afford the time, budget or resources to create original artwork. There may be times when it's more practical to use ready-made graphics, whether it's from your employer's image library, assets provided by a client, or images included within exercise files of a school assignment. There's nothing wrong with using outside resources to help you complete your design. But if you have a desire to learn how to draw, pursue it!

12. College is mandatory

I cannot express enough the importance of education. After all, education is necessary to advance in life, and is essential for career and personal growth. And, it's the key to successful development as a graphic designer. However, we receive education in many ways. So, while education is mandatory, college is not.

Let's be clear. I'm not here to discourage or dissuade anyone from going to college. In fact, I went to college myself…twice. Going to school may be the most beneficial route for some, but realistically it's not always the best solution for others. And, what many fail to realize is that it isn't the only solution to receiving a quality education and top-notch experience.

Believe it or not, many graphic designers are self-taught. A non-traditional way to learn, I know, but many graphic designers have actually created extremely successful careers for themselves. Whether you decide to learn graphic design at a college or university, or teach yourself, you are still acquiring your graphic design skills through learning. There's no way around that.

College is a wonderful opportunity, and experience is a great teacher. In fact, both can help up-and-coming graphic designers catapult their careers. But as I have mentioned before, you must have the drive and the passion to pursue a career in this industry. Both college and being self-taught require lots of hard work.

Still not sure which path to take? Well, let's examine each of these options so that you can consider which educational route is best for you.

College Route

There are many advantages to learning graphic design in a formal, educational setting. A worthy, comprehensive design program will provide structured learning; thoroughly teach the foundations of design (principles); provide hands-on training and tools; incorporate the latest and most relevant software; challenge you through diverse, thought-provoking assignments; and hopefully provide a good taste of "real world" projects.

A good design program will improve your technical proficiency, but even more so, it should increase your ability to think critically and solve problems creatively. In this environment, you are surrounded with others who are pursuing similar goals. You are submerged in an environment where there is healthy level of pressure to advance, and a support system of professors, teachers and/or assistants who can aid you through that process. In the end, you will earn a degree that will hopefully help take you to the next level: working in the "real world".

But, I must emphasize that you should not solely rely on your design degree to carry you through your career. Your degree will merely get you through the door. Experience through continued application of your skills will help you progress and grow as a designer. In other words, you need to keeping building on your experience by practicing, completing personal design projects, taking on freelance projects and/or gaining job experience.

Self-Taught Route
There are many advantages to learning design in an non-traditional manner, as well. Teaching yourself means that you can learn at your own pace and focus on the topics of interest to you. And more than likely, the price of your education won't be nearly as expensive as the price of college tuition. Some choose this route because they've already been to college or do not have the desire to pursue higher education. But for others, college may not be the right financial decision, or some may already work full time and are looking to transition to another career, needing the flexibility to learn on their own.

While those who are self-taught may not endure the rigors of a college classroom, they still must stick to a strict path of learning to gain the competencies needed to call themselves professional graphic designers. There must be an extreme drive, passion and determination to learn. Not only that, there needs to be a high level of commitment, discipline and consistency equal to if they were expected to go to class everyday. Fortunately, there are tons of resources out there to help if you decide to take this path, and because we live in the information age, there are many effective ways to engage in meaningful self-education practices. A few of them include:

- Online training sites (i.e. *lynda.com, tutsplus.com, treehouse.com*)
- Reputable accelerated programs that offer certification in different areas (i.e. The Iron Yard)
- Mentors, tutors and experienced graphic designers
- Design-related magazines for learning and inspiration (*HOW, Web Designer, CommArts*, and more)
- Websites, blogs and forums dedicated to graphic and/or web design-related topics (i.e. *smashingmagazine.com*)
- Meetup groups or clubs focusing on graphic design
- Good ole' books (remember those?) from the bookstore or library

MYTH: COLLEGE IS MANDATORY

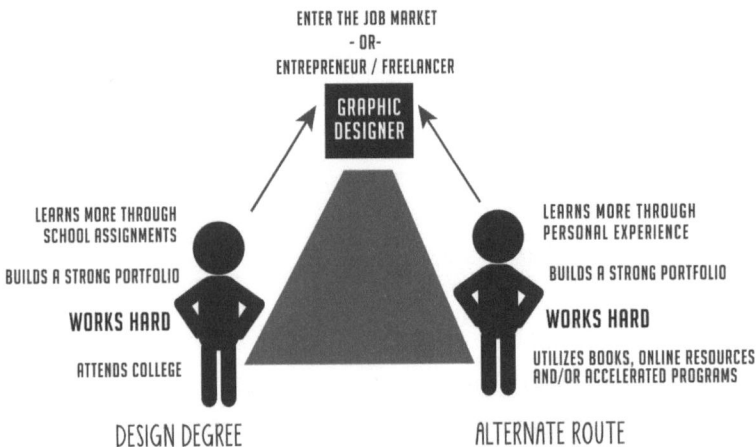

ENTER THE JOB MARKET
- OR-
ENTREPRENEUR / FREELANCER

GRAPHIC DESIGNER

LEARNS MORE THROUGH SCHOOL ASSIGNMENTS

LEARNS MORE THROUGH PERSONAL EXPERIENCE

BUILDS A STRONG PORTFOLIO

BUILDS A STRONG PORTFOLIO

WORKS HARD

WORKS HARD

ATTENDS COLLEGE

UTILIZES BOOKS, ONLINE RESOURCES AND/OR ACCELERATED PROGRAMS

DESIGN DEGREE

ALTERNATE ROUTE

I can personally attest to the advantages of both forms of education. I learned the foundations of graphic design, had tons of practice, and made decent strides using design software during my undergraduate studies. However, web design was something that I taught myself over time after college. I first developed a real interest to learn web design when I started applying to full-time jobs after graduating. My first real web design project was creating a personal portfolio website from scratch to help increase my chances of landing a job. Then down the road, I continued to push myself to learn more web design techniques— like CSS, content management systems and familiarizing myself with other programming languages — to keep up with the demands of my freelance clients. I even remember a former co-worker giving me a crash course on CSS during one of our lunch breaks! It has certainly been a discovery process of trial and error. But honestly, for me, trial and error proved to be one of my best methods of learning because I began to understand what worked, what didn't, and why.

In 2009, I also ended up pursuing a graduate certificate program to learn interactive design and Flash (if only I knew then that in a few years Flash would be on the brink of extinction within the web design world...oh well). Again, I learned many foundational principles about interactive design, and I reaped the benefits of the school's resources and being around other students who had the same interests. Now, I'm revisiting web design technologies and beginning to learn on my own how I can integrate this new knowledge with my design skills to stay on top of the game. There have even been opportunities for me to learn video editing and motion graphics on my own through job requests or freelance projects. That just goes to show that learning can come in many forms, but still be effective.

Employment vs. Entrepreneurship
If your goal is to work for someone else, whether it's a corporation, non-profit organization, creative agency or government, be aware that in some cases, a degree of some sort will be required. Sometimes companies require a Bachelor's degree in general, while others specifically require some type of degree in design or a related field. While it is not impossible to get your foot in the door without a degree, know that you will need:

1) A great level of design experience and/or proficiency, and
2) An awesome portfolio to prove it.

Remember, even without a degree, a graphic designer can be just as good as those with degrees. However, be aware of those employers that require a degree and those that don't.

If you want to work for yourself — say establishing your own design firm, becoming an app developer, or just using your design skills to help build your own business — then whether or not you obtain a degree is really up to you. If you know that you need a structured learning environment and feel that a particular program at a college or university is the right program for you, then that's great! However, if you are more apt to learn on your own, have already done the college thing (and student loans), and/or are interested in alternative ways of learning graphic design, then you can make it without college and a degree.

Again, the emphasis is on learning. No matter how you've learned or who you've learned it from, the most important thing is that you find a way to learn what you need to advance and grow as a designer. Within that learning process, surround yourself with those who can properly guide you in the right direction. But, choose the path that makes the most sense for your situation. There's no right or wrong way…only the way that's most effective for you.

13. Being creative is easy

It was a hot summer night. I was staring at the computer, and it was staring back at me. A blank look was plastered on my face as the time continued to tick away. My final project — probably one of the hardest assignments I had ever been tasked with — was for a graduate course and was due promptly at 9 a.m. But, it was 2 a.m., and I still wasn't done. While this might sound like a story of procrastination — and it partly is — it's more of a story about creative struggle.

The assignment was to create a video game design document, expanding on an original video game concept and detailing the storyline, levels, characters and scoring elements. In actuality, I hadn't waited until the last minute to start working on this project, but every time I would sit down to work on it, I would get so flustered with having to come up with so much creative content on my own. Even after figuring out a general direction that I wanted to go in, the idea of having to write a story, draw characters and scenery AND put it all together in a nicely designed document became overwhelming. I felt that I could only exert so much brainpower on it at a time, and when I would hit a wall with writing the next part of the game, everything else took a hit, too.

Needless to say, after a few cans of Red Bull and an entire pack of Thin Mints (bad idea, trust me), I pulled an all-nighter, and thankfully, I was able to finish. But, I don't think I ever struggled that much to extract my creativity.

There are those who have the misconception that creating an amazing design is easy. To the untrained eye, using just the right amount of white space, understanding when to keep it simple and when to dial it up, creating harmony between fonts and imagery, creating a powerful color palette, or using just the right level of contrast are elements that always seem to just fall into place. But, it's not always that easy.

In fact, creativity takes work. There's not a magic wand or a light bulb that blinks above your head with a creative idea. There is no creative cheat sheet. When you are challenged to dream up something big, it will take a good amount of thought, planning and patience. It's not an easy task to just make something up, have that concept make sense, and make it look good, all at the same time.

Yes, it is true that some people have the natural gift of creativity. And yes, there are moments of inspiration where the stars are aligned, the gears are turning, and you can release your creativity with no inhibitions. Those times when you are truly in your "creative zone" are priceless, and you can create some of your best work. But, those ingenious moments won't always show up upon request.

If you are tasked with coming up with an idea, and you can't immediately think of something great, it's okay. Be patient with yourself, and give yourself a chance to think. Sometimes you may just hit a wall, but other times, you may just need more information about the project or better insight. If you are tired, in a distracting environment, or your willpower is low, finding creativity can also be extremely difficult.

But there are ways to help you move through your creative block. When you are faced with creative struggles:

- Try looking at other creative examples for inspiration. Skim through design magazines or books, Google some key words, check out design blogs/sites, look back at some of your old work, or study someone else's work to help generate some new ideas.
- Discuss the problem you're trying to solve with someone else to get a different perspective. Feed off of others' ideas.
- Listen to music. This is a good way to relax your mind or amp you up.
- Refresh and renew your mind by changing your environment. Take a walk to clear your head, and refresh your thoughts so that you can think at your best.
- Do something totally unrelated to design. Play a video game. Cook. Go watch a movie. Take a nap. Run through a field and catch butterflies. Whatever. Just take your mind off the task at hand for a bit. You'll discover that design inspiration can come at the most random moments!

So the next time you have a hard time coming up with something creative, just take a deep breath, remembering that the inspiration will come.

14. There's only one way

Have you ever heard the phrase, "There's more than one way to skin a cat"? Well, there's definitely more than one way to reach a solution in graphic design. Because we have different ways of thinking about the world and different levels of understanding, it is no surprise that, as designers, we sometimes might approach the same challenges with different solutions.

For example, consider the list of tasks below. How would you go about creating each one? What design software would you use?

- Create a 8.5-in. x 11-in. flyer
- Create a business card
- Create a home page design for a website
- Create a login screen design for a mobile app
- Create a four-page sell sheet

Now, let's think about this list of common design techniques. How would you execute each of these?

- Copy and paste a singular object
- Create a new design file
- Change the color of a logo
- Modify the size of a page layout
- Change text from one font to another

When considering how to accomplish these tasks, I'm pretty sure that no one will have the same answers. One designer might create a flyer in InDesign while another may create it in Photoshop. A website design concept might be best accomplished in Photoshop while others may find Illustrator will work best. There are multiple ways to do the same task and get the same results! But, as you grow and continue to learn, you will discover that certain software programs are better suited for certain tasks. For example, when I first started designing, I used Photoshop to do everything — and I do mean everything. One day, I got a request from a client to scale up a logo I had created, wanting it much bigger than the original size I had created using Photoshop. The problem was that I wasn't able to scale it up without it becoming extremely pixelated (blurry). I later learned that creating all my logos as vectors in Illustrator would be best so that scalability would not be an issue.

As you continue in design, you'll learn by intention — or by accident — that you can do a single function in two or three different ways within your software programs. Some ways might be faster, more efficient, or more precise than the way you were doing it before. For example, you might create a new design file by going to the File menu and selecting "New", or you might just use the keyboard shortcut Cmd/Cntrl N.

Just keep an open mind, and be willing to try new ways of accomplishing your tasks. After all, your peers, your boss or your teacher may ask you to do the same task in completely different ways. That's not to say that either of you is right or wrong per se, but it does allow you to evaluate which way might be better for what you're trying to accomplish. You'll also begin to learn best practices for optimizing your time and your skills by using the proper software and techniques that will be the most efficient.

COPYING AND PASTING

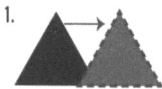

1.

SELECT OBJECT WITH CURSOR.
EDIT > COPY
EDIT > PASTE

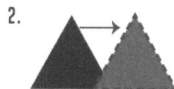

2.

SELECT OBJECT WITH CURSOR.
TYPE CMD/CTRL C
THEN TYPE CMD/CTRL C

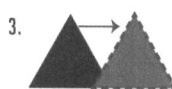

3.

SELECT OBJECT WITH CURSOR.

HOLD DOWN THE ALT KEY UNTIL A WHITE ARROW APPEARS IN FRONT OF THE BLACK SELECTION ARROW.

DRAG THE OBJECT (WHILE STILL HOLDING THE ALT KEY) AND ITS DUPLICATE WILL APPEAR.

Remember, there's more than one way to design. Take advantage of those moments when you discover something new. What might seem like an accidental keystroke or menu click could very well turn into your new trick! And, remember to share what you learn with others!

15. Software will design for you

Have you noticed hardware innovations like the revolutionary "design" button that will be featured on select laptops and desktop computer brands? Did you read the reviews about the upcoming "create" feature you can use with any software simply by typing a series of special codes?

Of course you didn't. That's because those features don't exist. Software programs, like those within the Adobe Creative Suite, are powerful tools. Productions houses for movies, television studios, national magazines and renowned designers use some of the same software programs that you might be using. So that must mean that good software automatically produces good design, right? Nope.

Software programs are powerful tools. Professional design software can produce extremely high-level work when the person using it possesses the necessary skills to take full advantage of its tools. Yet, those same software programs have limited influence without a true understanding of good design. In all, the most powerful tool you will use is your mind.

Think of these programs as extensions of your creativity and the avenues by which you execute your ideas. Although you may gain some inspiration while experimenting with some of the tools, design programs will not generate ideas for you. They only carry out the vision in your mind and the skill of your hands. After all, a state-of-the-art kitchen is useless if you don't know a thing about cooking. The fastest, sleekest sports car has a lot of horsepower, but only when it's driven. Similarly, design software was never made to do all of the work for you.

MYTH: SOFTWARE WILL DESIGN FOR YOU

"ALAKAZAM...CREATE COOL POSTER NOW!"

As you work to improve your software skills, you should work to improve your thinking skills even more. Ask yourself, "What am I really trying to do? What functions do I want my design to have, and how should they look? What software can I use to achieve the best results?" Anyone can learn how to push buttons and click around in a program. But having the ability to formulate meaningful design solutions and translate them well using software will distinguish the true designers from the rest.

5 TRUTHS

No matter the designer, there are just some things that apply to us all. Find out what we all have in common.

16. You might suck (for a little while)

I don't know about you, but the first time I opened Adobe Illustrator, I felt like I stepped into a nightmare. I just stared at the screen for about 10 minutes because I had no idea where to start. I think I drew a circle or two. But eventually, with frustration, I clicked File > Close. I had enough.

Starting something new can be challenging and a bit intimidating. As you begin to learn graphic design principles and start experimenting with various design software programs, you will experience a learning curve or the "struggle curve" as I call it. You might navigate around design programs with incredible ease, but maybe you have not quite grasped what makes good design. Or, you might have a pretty good handle on design principles but struggle to understand how to make a design come to life using software. Perhaps there is a knowledge gap, misinformation, lack of experience, or even intimidation that stifles your quality of work in the early stages.

When I was first introduced to graphic design about 15 years ago, I was already pretty artistic and fairly decent with technology. Well, let's just say I knew how to e-mail a Word document and how to scribble using the paint program that came with my computer. But I didn't know how to design. At least, I didn't know how to design *well*. I had a lot of great ideas stored in my head, but I had no idea what to do to make those ideas a reality.

Although I had my fair share of frustrations, I really liked design, and I was determined to stick it out and see where the journey would take me. Eventually, with continued education, persistence and lots of practice, I improved each year. I even mustered up the courage to start freelancing in college.

Looking back on some of my early work, I chuckle and wonder, "Someone paid me for this? Wow, this really stinks!" I'm humbled that my first paid clients were willing to give me a chance. I mean, the work wasn't terrible. But it definitely didn't need to go on display either! But what I learned is that I had to start somewhere. The same goes for you, too.

YOU MIGHT SUCK (FOR A LITTLE WHILE)

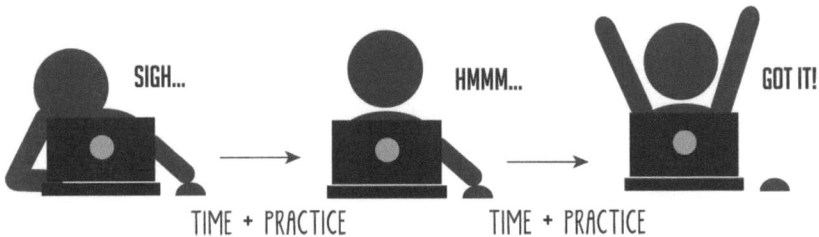

SIGH...   HMMM...   GOT IT!

TIME + PRACTICE   TIME + PRACTICE

Your design work five years from now, two years from now, or even six months from now will be greatly improved from when you first started. Even your skill level, productivity and confidence will increase. But, you must make a sincere effort to really work at it. I have made mistakes...lots of mistakes. And, I'm still making mistakes today. But I learned from them and improved. You will make mistakes, too, and yes, you may even suck for a little while. But that's okay. Some things will come easy to you and others won't. That is a normal part of the learning and growing process. You will get better. Anything worthwhile is worth doing — no matter if you are good or bad at it in the beginning!

17. You should NEVER stop learning

Great minds never stop learning. So that means great designers don't stop learning either. No matter where you go to school, where you work, who mentors you, or how many years of design experience you have, you will never know everything. If you think you know everything now, you don't!

It's easy to become comfortable once you think you've reached a certain skill level, found the best and only way to accomplish a design task, or fail to explore other design-related avenues.

LEARNING NEVER STOPS

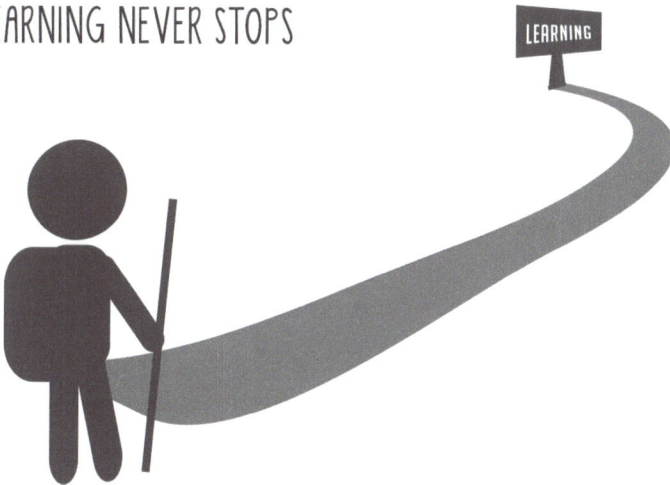

LEARNING

I know a few graphic designers who are gurus in print design and branding, but have not delved into web design — either because they just haven't taken the time to learn it, it seemed too difficult, or they just weren't interested. Some of them were even presented with employment opportunities that required web design experience or they were approached by freelance clients who needed web design. But because they didn't have the knowledge to tackle those types of projects, they were forced to turn them down, missing out on good opportunities and good money. I'm not saying that every graphic designer must become an expert in web design, but I am saying that you should always keep learning, even if you enhance the skills that you already have.

Although you won't be able to master every aspect of graphic design, familiarizing yourself with other areas will enhance your skills. For example, while you may enjoy creating signage and large format layouts, you can learn about designing more intricate and extensive layouts as well, in the event that you are asked to work on something of a smaller, more text-heavy format. In addition, while your specialty may be print design, gaining a few skills designing for the web may help if you ever collaborate with a web designer. You might just even surprise yourself, and decide to pursue this new path full time.

Here's another reason to keep learning. Graphic design is such a fast-paced and growing profession, and if you don't keep up with technological advances and the latest design trends, you — and your designs — will be left in the dust.

Here are a few things to keep learning about:

Software and updates
Technology changes quickly, so you will always need to pay attention to the software that's out there. Figure out what software works best for the tasks you need to accomplish, and continue to become proficient in those you use everyday. Always look for new tools that can help you with your design workflow and proficiency.

Hardware

While you don't need the latest and greatest laptop or phone to be an effective designer, you will need decent tools to stay current in the industry. I personally have a MacBook, but I find it useful to work on both Mac and PC systems for various reasons. One reason is that certain software programs may only be available on one platform and not the other. Learn what devices work best for the type of design you do, and make sure that your hardware is equipped to run current design software and connect to other modern devices.

Breaking design news

Learn about what is going on in the design world. Success stories, failures, new technological advances, and articles highlighting companies or individuals within your industry are great to read. They are informative, but you'll find that they are also inspiring and encouraging.

Design trends

Learn about the techniques that are in and which ones are not. Overuse of bevels, embossing, drop shadows and clip art were gold in the '90s but not so cool in the 21st century. Having an awareness of design trends doesn't mean that you have to follow them, but it is important to know what visual cues are currently used in popular culture.

New web standards

The web changes so rapidly, and there are always new standards, frameworks, content management tools, programming languages and software emerging. Remember when the Internet was known as the Information Superhighway? Or when SEO wasn't a big deal? What about when Flash websites were the hottest thing since sliced bread? Maybe you do or maybe you don't, but that shows how rapidly the web has evolved. Ever-changing web standards will affect the way you design, how you approach a project (depending on its requirements), and what solutions you will implement.

New print technologies
If you are a graphic designer who primarily focuses on print design, you should stay abreast of any improved pre-flighting techniques (checking your file to make sure it's print-ready), growth and development of print processes, new papers and inks, and more efficient practices. You may even be interested in more eclectic printing practices, like 3D printing.

....

There will always be something to learn and discover. And, the reasons to keep learning — improving your skills; workplace, classroom or business growth; increased job security; opportunities to earn more income — are endless. Particularly in the design field, constant learning and skill improvement is very important. Now is not the time to create a ceiling for your achievement. Don't close your mind to new ways of thinking, and don't rely on your past success to guide your future. Sure, it's okay to celebrate your successes but do not — I repeat, DO NOT — stop learning. Why limit yourself? Keep learning and striving to be the best designer you can be.

18. You should build an awesome portfolio

I remember going to a job interview and lugging around my big, bulky and slightly worn portfolio. With sweaty palms and butterflies in my stomach, I nervously waited for the interviewer to ask me a bunch of unrealistic and awkward what-would-you-do-if questions. Instead she said, "Let's skip over all the boring talk and get straight to the good stuff. I want to see your work!"

Since you are going to be creating some pretty awesome designs, you need to be able to show them off! As you continue to create new design pieces and work on various projects, keep your portfolio in mind. At some point, you will need to show your work to nail a job interview, apply to an academic program, persuade a prospective client, or maybe even enter a design contest. No matter the situation, you should frequently think about how you can successfully build your awesome design portfolio.

The key word here is "awesome". Your portfolio needs to be awesome and nothing less. In essence, it's your visual resume. Your design portfolio is not for all of your work — it's only reserved for your best work!

Now you're probably asking, "What if I don't have any design work yet? What if I don't have much to show? What if I have too much work and can't choose what to use?"

If you are new to design, and you don't have any projects or you don't have anything that you wouldn't be too embarrassed to show, that's okay. Just keep designing! If you haven't designed anything yet or don't have any client work, school design projects or anything "real" to work on, make something up! Create a logo for an imaginary company, or be proactive and make a flyer for your church or a community event. Create an opportunity to design something great. If you keep designing, by default, you will end up with a pool of work from which to choose. But again, choose the work you're most proud of for your portfolio.

If you do have a lot of design work but can't seem to decide what stands out as your best, then consider these few pointers:

- **Your portfolio should be a reflection of your best work.** If your initial response to certain pieces is

"Eh", followed by a shoulder shrug, then take them out of the running.

- **There is no magic number for how many portfolio pieces you need to have.** But when deciding what pieces you will include, you definitely shouldn't have too many or too few. You don't want to overwhelm the viewer with too many pieces but you also don't want to underwhelm them by not having enough. Imagine yourself explaining each and every one of your portfolio pieces to someone. How much or how little time would that take?
- **Try to keep your portfolio diverse.** If you have some great examples showcasing different styles or different types of work, then mix it up and show your versatility. In other words, if you've got great samples of a web design, a brochure, a sign and a logo, that's more effective than five different business card designs. Show that you can excel in more than one area of design, if possible.
- **Show designs that reflect the style your client is seeking, and give priority to those designs.** For example, if you are applying to a magazine publishing company, show samples that highlight your layout skills rather than showing a sketch that you drew of your dog.

One of the benefits of carrying your work in a physical portfolio is that you can pull out tangible print samples and put them in someone's hand. This is especially effective if you want to show off the final production of your work — maybe a really nice brochure, a catalogue you worked on, or the texture of a cool marketing piece.

The alternative to a physical portfolio is an online portfolio, which, I think, is important for every designer to have (even if you already have a physical portfolio). Online portfolios can be accessed just about anywhere, are easy to update, can include written descriptions of each piece, and obviously, much more work can be displayed than what you could probably carry in a physical portfolio. Sometimes it's just more convenient to send someone a link to your online portfolio or attach your work to an e-mail.

Portfolio items can be posted on a self-hosted site or you can choose from a variety of online portfolio services, blogs, or forums. As an alternative, you could create interactive PDFs or archive a collection of jpegs that capture your work. There's really no right or wrong way to put your portfolio together. As you can see, there's so many ways to display your work in a creative, professional manner. Just make sure you are showcasing your best work in a way that is easily viewable to your audience.

19. Details matter

I got a lot of "A-minuses" on my design projects in college. This may sound great to you, but the "minus" part always drove me crazy! I always wondered, why not just a solid "A"? Later, while working at my first full-time design job, I once found myself sitting in an empty, halfway-lit office building — on a Saturday afternoon no less — frantically fixing a file after the printer guy e-mailed me about some error he found while running the press. On a separate occasion, I had worked on a really nice direct mail piece that was sent to thousands of customers. Only later did I find out that there was a misspelled word on every last one of them!

So, what do all those scenarios have in common? The details.

As you begin your design journey, you will discover that the details really do matter. If you think they don't, ask a surgeon who is performing a life-saving surgery, or an engineer who is building a complex bridge over which millions of cars will drive. Consider a baker whose recipe requires a very specific amount of flour to pull off an intricate pastry. The details, in fact, do matter.

Unfortunately, there were details in each of these situations that were overlooked, and I suffered the consequences. I discovered that designers who fail to pay attention to those details are guaranteed to do at least one of two things:

1) Produce error-trodden designs — and some of those errors could be expensive!
2) Produce mediocre designs that lack finesse and character.

You don't want to be classified as an average designer or the one who always makes mistakes. Part of being a great graphic designer is giving just as much attention to the small things as the big things. Small things sound unimportant, but everything in your design is important! After all, it is all of those details — the thin strokes that outline a graphic, the alignment of elements on a page, the correct spelling/grammar of words, the intricacy of illustrations, the time you take to properly Photoshop an image, or the effective pairing of fonts used on a website — that work together to elevate a design from "okay" to "great".

Details can be categorized in two ways. There are intentional details that you purposely build into your design, and there are details classified as errors that you should work to improve upon or eliminate all together.

Intentional details
Adding that extra level of "finesse" to your design can often be attributed to the details. Imagine a plain, yellow cake with no icing. Now imagine a gourmet birthday cake, piped with delicate

DETAILS MATTER

OK DESIGN   **GREAT DESIGN**

icing patterns, layered with perfectly sliced strawberries along the sides and your name written in fancy script on the top. Which cake looks more detailed and therefore is more eye-catching and appealing?

Don't confuse detail with being elaborate or over the top. Just because you add more "stuff" to your design doesn't mean that it's better. The key is to add detail where it can enhance the overall presentation, give more meaning to the message, or provide more emphasis to important elements. Becoming cognizant of good design principles and fine-tuning your approach through details makes a difference.

Corrective details

There will be many times when you will catch little things — incorrect spelling, an extra something floating in the corner, the wrong font, inconsistent graphic elements — that weren't meant to live in your design. Having the ability to spot and correct these details is invaluable.

But, it's not just design elements that you need to consider. Make sure, among other things, that you are saving your work in the correct file format, removing unnecessary elements in the file, making comments where necessary (when writing code), and naming files and layers in a way that makes sense.

....

Having an awareness of these details will be become easier over time, so don't worry. Just remember that details are everywhere, and they should not be ignored. Be intentional in adding details where appropriate and correcting them when necessary. Remember that details separate the mediocre designs from the extraordinary ones.

20. You are your own brand

Your job as a graphic designer is to develop innovative ideas, create cool designs, fill in the creative gaps that your clients may lack, and help build brands for other people. But did you know that at the same time, you are building your own brand, too? As you continue to learn, grow and build your portfolio of work, don't forget to build the brand of YOU.

Brands are complex because they not only consist of a name and logo, but they also encompass other elements: taglines, unique sounds, imagery, colors, scents, movements and perceptions, just to name a few. As an individual, your design style, work ethic, personality and the traits that make you unique are all working together in the background to develop your personal brand — whether you intended them to or not. The designer and business person that people will perceive you to be is often a direct reflection of how you are building the brand of "You" over time. What do you want people to think about you as a designer?

"He's the go-to guy if you want something done quick, fast, and in a hurry."

"She's very thorough in her thought process and building out of ideas."

"He works great with everyone."

"She's not really a people person, but she can get the job done."

"I like working with him because his files are always clean and organized when he passes them off to me."

WHAT'S YOUR PERSONAL BRAND?

Some of the factors that will contribute to your personal brand are:

Your design style

Many designers develop a design style or niche over the course of time. You might be known as the designer who designs "clean and simple", or you might be classified as the "artsy" designer or the "avant-garde" designer. I can assure you that you definitely don't want to be the "boring" designer. Maybe you like using a particular color palette or font type more than others, or perhaps your designs are very ambitious and over the top. Whatever your design style, at some point, others will begin to recognize it.

Your integrity and work ethic

Are you honest in your work? Do you give credit where credit is
due? Can people trust you to carry out their ideas successfully?
Are others comfortable working with you? Are you diligent
in providing fair pricing or accurately counting the hours you
worked on a project? Do you work hard or do just enough to get
by? Your work ethic plays a big role in your personal brand and
how others will perceive you.

The way you work with others

It's inevitable. You're going to have to work with other people,
whether it's clients, employers or other designers. There's no way
around that. Strive to make those experiences as pleasurable and
effective as possible. Collaborate with other designers to the best
of your ability and create your files in a way that another designer
could successfully work from, especially in the event that you
need to pass off your work to someone else. Do your best to
communicate well with your clients, employers or teachers. That
means clearly articulating and explaining your designs, taking
direction and criticism, and learning how to find that happy
medium where everyone — including you — is satisfied with the
quality of your work.

The standards you set for yourself

What's important to you? How far do you want to go as a
designer? What are your goals or ambitions? The value of your
brand increases when you strive to be the best designer that you
can be. Continue to set high standards for yourself and always
continue on a path of learning and self-improvement. When
you are confident in the value of your work, you can become
a force to be reckoned with! Even with the rise of people who
have no aptitude for design dabbling more into designer territory
and gaining access to online tools and software, those strides
ultimately cannot replace the aptitude of designers who know
their worth and have built strong personal brands.

As you continue to discover who you are as a designer, don't be afraid to make mistakes. Mistakes provide great opportunities to learn and make improvements. Your personal brand is not about striving for perfection, but more about becoming the best "you" that you can be.

So, no matter where you decide to work or with whom you decide to work, you will always carry your personal brand — those unique qualities that make you an awesome designer!

5

OTHER THINGS

A few "extras" that all graphic designers should do!

21. You should freelance. Seriously.

Freelancing is something that every designer should try at least once. This topic is worthy of its own book, but we'll just cover the basics. Wikipedia defines a freelancer as "a person who is self-employed and is not committed to a particular employer long-term." I define it as independently taking on client projects full time, part time or as desired.

For some, it can be a gateway to self-employment or become a hobby. But others find out it's just not for them. Whether you're in school, work a nine-to-five job, or are looking to work for yourself full time, freelancing is a challenge to take on at some point. It's worth a try to discover what it can do for you. Here's why:

Experience and Grow
One reason you should explore freelance opportunities is that you will have the chance to develop your skills through unique experiences. Sure, you can gain design experience from school or a job. In fact, a large chunk of your design experience might come from school or work assignments. But there's something about handling your own design projects that puts freelance experiences in a league of their own. Freelance projects are a bit uninhibited and less predictable than the workload you might be used to at school or at a job, and these projects innately have a greater potential to be more versatile and challenging than those strategically assigned to you. You can, after all, seek out your own work and control the level at which you do those jobs.

My own school assignments — while creative and challenging — introduced me to the design industry. And, my on-the-job experiences in the corporate world tested my ability to think quickly, work with various team members and clients, and required me to adapt to certain processes and procedures. But, it's the projects that I have done for myself that have been the most fulfilling, interesting and thought-provoking. Through freelancing, I was able to try new types of design projects beyond what I was used to, work on ideas that I really believed in, attempt new design styles, and challenge myself by working with diverse clients. Freelance projects took me out of my comfort zone, which I sometimes found myself in while working on school or work projects.

Yes, freelancing can help you become a better designer. But you will hopefully become a better businessperson, too. Of course your core responsibility will be design. But freelancing will encourage you to wear more than one hat. For example, you will be managing client relations (making phone calls, e-mail communications, coordinating meetings), handling finances (billing clients, keeping financial records organized, and budgeting out projects), selling your services (pitching ideas to clients, putting in bids for potential work), and coordinating marketing efforts (advertising your services, finding ways to stay relevant in the market).

You'll also be afforded the opportunity to add new skills, improve those skills you already have, and become better at delivering your projects on time, making clients happy, and building a name for yourself. Like anything else, when you first start — similar to this design journey that you are just beginning — you won't have all the answers, and it may be somewhat intimidating. But with each freelance project you complete, you'll have a better understanding of how you can improve the next experience. With persistence and an open mind to learn and change when necessary, your freelance projects can become some of the most valuable and fulfilling projects you will ever have.

Make money

Another reason designers often choose to freelance is the opportunity to make money. While you may choose to offer your freelance work for free, most freelancers actually generate an income from their work. It's an opportunity to do what they love while also getting paid.

If you are a beginner, inexperienced or "learning as you go", consider getting your feet wet first by taking on a few "pro-bono" freelance projects before you begin charging clients. In these cases, the payoffs you will receive are experience and exposure. You just need to be clear on how much "free" work you're willing to do and for whom.

As you make your way through the ranks, you'll learn what rates, pricing structures and policies work best for you. Consider your current level of experience and expertise, the competitive rates of your direct competitors, and of course, the scope of work and time constraints given for requested projects. It can be somewhat complicated — some experienced designers still struggle to find their comfort zone in pricing — but you just have to be accountable and make your pricing fair. And, your design services should maintain a quality standard that reflects those prices.

Make Discoveries

You really like logo design, but you hate laying out brochures. You enjoy web design and have no interest in print design. You'd rather work with small businesses than with large corporations. You'd like to charge hourly rather than charging a flat rate, or vice versa. These are the types of discoveries you will make when you seek out your own projects. You may discover that you like being your own boss and you want to start working at your own design business full time. Or you may discover that freelancing just isn't for you, and you work best under the direction of an employer.

Whatever direction you choose is up to you, but make sure that you make informed decisions based on your own experiences and discoveries...not on others' opinions.

Diversify

Freelancing offers one of the fastest ways to diversify your portfolio. Why? You have the opportunity to work with different types of clients with different needs, which will often result in diverse design projects. Let's say you get bored with the same type of projects at work, or you feel that your job isn't utilizing your talents to their fullest potential. Freelance work is a great way to fill the void.

Fail to Succeed

A few years ago, I had one of the craziest client experiences ever. My business partner and I were commissioned to design an identity package — which included a logo, business cards and full website — for a client. We were all excited to get started. Our client was eager to get his ideas rolling, and we were glad to help. The income we would receive would be pretty nice, too.

The project started smoothly, and at first, everything seemed to happen according to plan. But eventually, our communication with the client began to dwindle over the following weeks. We were determined to continue working and maintain a decent timeline, but reaching the client became more difficult. Despite the breakdown in communication, we managed to complete most of the projects and have the items approved. There was, however, one final item: a website draft. We completed the website design for review, and notified the client via phone and e-mail that the draft was complete. No response. After several more attempts to contact the client, there was still no response.

Then one night, my business partner noticed a missed call on his phone. The client left a vile voicemail message, claiming he hadn't received any work from us since we started the project, and he threatened to sue! He also demanded we refund ALL of his money the next morning even though the majority of the work had already been completed. Of course, our heads were spinning. After replaying his message a few times and still in disbelief, my business partner gave the client a call, which quickly became a heated, non-"G-rated" conversation. But eventually, the issue was resolved.

So, what happened to all of the e-mails we sent for the client's approval?

Interestingly, the client reluctantly checked his e-mail and — Bam! The website link we e-mailed weeks ago had been sitting in his inbox. Not only that, but he absolutely "loved" the website once he finally saw it. But by that point, his praise wasn't enough to undo the scars of his crazy rant.

That experience wasn't an ideal situation by any means. In fact, some might consider it an absolute failure. Maybe it was. But, we learned from it. Yes, we learned to never, ever work with that guy again, but we also discovered that failure is a part of learning.

I imagine many designers avoid freelancing for this very reason. The idea of failing isn't an easy one to digest. But, don't let the "F" word scare you. Instead of approaching failure as a point of no return, think of it as a lesson. As you begin tackling new projects, working with new clients, and figuring out how to balance your workload, you must understand that you will make mistakes. And, you will have failures. But once you accept that, you won't be intimidated by failure any longer. Even the most successful entrepreneurs have many failures, but those failures were the pathway to their successes.

The key to failure is not just about learning what went wrong, but actually applying what you've learned and moving in a better, smarter direction. By failing, you'll learn what and what not to say; what and what not to do; the types of projects to take on and those you will leave behind; and what people you enjoy working with and those you would rather not work with again. In addition, you'll learn what pricing rates work and those that don't; what projects are worth your time; language that should be in your contracts or work agreements; and what processes (and people) don't mix well with your workflow. You may even discover that you really don't have a system at all. As you continue freelancing, all of these lessons will come, some more quickly than others. The beauty of failure is the wisdom and understanding that follows when you can truly extract the lessons from those situations. So remember, if you're not failing, you're not succeeding!

ANATOMY OF A FREELANCER

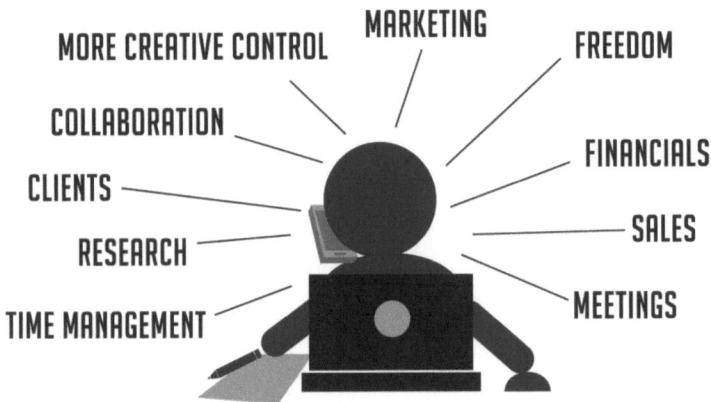

MORE CREATIVE CONTROL MARKETING FREEDOM
COLLABORATION FINANCIALS
CLIENTS SALES
RESEARCH
TIME MANAGEMENT MEETINGS

Freelancing can present some great opportunities. When you are ready, take that step, and try a small freelance project. Then keep building from there. You can do it on your own, or you can team up with other designers. Everyone's formula for success is different, so freelance in the way that works best for you. You will either love it or learn from it. Either way, do it!

Disclaimer: Be sure that your freelance work is not a conflict of interest with your employment or schoolwork. Also, gauge how much you can handle and how you will be ethical and responsible in your execution.

22. Don't take it personal

Although I was never that fond of the design critiques I had to endure in college, they were necessary. In most cases, the design critiques I experienced in school involved each student standing in front of the class with his/her project on display and explaining the thought process behind the design that was created. The teacher and other students were then free to ask questions, tell you what they liked, what they didn't like, or that you should think of another idea altogether.

And yes, there was always that one person that nit-picked everything. Why this? Why that? There were times when I honestly didn't have a justifiable response to why I designed the way I did, so I would just muster up some half-baked explanation. But, with each critique, I began to realize that not only should I be prepared to justify my design choices, but I also realized the value in the feedback I received. My teachers and classmates often pointed out inconsistencies in my layout, typographical errors and little details that I would have never noticed or considered. They also gave great suggestions that could help improve my designs.

Wouldn't it be terrible if someone saw a flaw in your design and instead of pointing it out to help you, they just smiled, nodded, and let you continue to make mistakes? Constructive criticism is valuable and necessary, and should be welcomed for greater improvement in a designer's work. And, if it hasn't already happened, at some point, it will. Inevitably, there will be someone who isn't going to like something you created. You will be asked to fix, edit or rethink your design. You may even be asked to start over.

DON'T TAKE IT PERSONAL

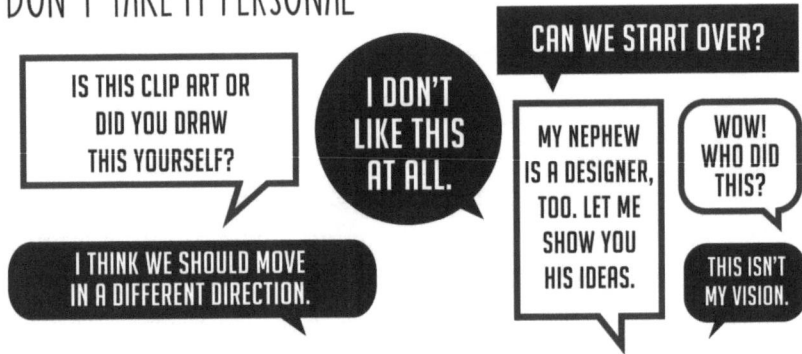

CAN WE START OVER?

IS THIS CLIP ART OR DID YOU DRAW THIS YOURSELF?

I DON'T LIKE THIS AT ALL.

MY NEPHEW IS A DESIGNER, TOO. LET ME SHOW YOU HIS IDEAS.

WOW! WHO DID THIS?

I THINK WE SHOULD MOVE IN A DIFFERENT DIRECTION.

THIS ISN'T MY VISION.

Don't take it personal. The key is to be open-minded and receptive to constructive criticism, and accept that everything you create won't be "right" on the first attempt. In fact, there are no designers with a perfect track record, and you most likely won't have one either. The design critique will help you to recognize your weaknesses so that you grow and get better.

In addition to receiving critiques from others, the ability to use objective judgment when evaluating your own design is also important. The real beauty is when you can, on your own, point out flaws or errors in your designs, or recognize the areas where you can improve.

So, put on your thick skin now! Understand that constructive feedback is good, and criticism of your work is not personal (well, it shouldn't be). Constructive criticism and feedback is just as much a part of the design process as the creation of your work.

But what if you feel the feedback you receive is not legitimate? Over the course of your design career, you will receive criticism that seems petty or comments that are unsubstantiated. You have to be able to differentiate between the two, using your overall understanding of design. Try asking yourself some of these helpful questions about criticism:

- **Is it considering a technical, logistical or content-based change?** ("This word is spelled wrong." "The wrong logo was used." "The imagery used doesn't represent the brand.")
- **Does it help you better align your design with the overall message, or does it help the audience more clearly understand the message?** ("This information is important, but the font size is too small to read." "The layout is confusing." "The images tell a different story than what was intended.")
- **Does it align with the fundamentals of design principles?** ("There really isn't enough contrast." "The colors used aren't working with the overall tone." "There are too many decorative elements that take away from the actual purpose of the design.")
- **Does it help you creatively solve the problem in a more effective manner?** ("This should be a brochure instead of a one-page flyer." "There needs to be a call to action." "This design doesn't speak to the audience in a way they would understand.")

Learn how to recognize legitimate feedback, whether you want to hear it or not. When analyzing feedback, you must have the ability to either refute it by defending your design decisions, come to a compromise that all parties can live with, or graciously accept the criticism and heed to the changes. With time and experience, separating meaningful feedback from subjective, hollow comments will become much easier.

Don't let your ego, or your need to be "right", artistically free and uninhibited stand in the way of accepting criticism. Learn to take advice from designers who may have valuable experience, tips or lessons to share with you. Appreciate the honesty of your peers and clients, and use that criticism to improve your execution. You'll be thankful for it in the end.

23. Make other graphic design friends

The summer before my freshman year of college, I had the opportunity to choose who would be my roommate for the upcoming school year. I had the seemingly random choice between two girls I had never met, so because I didn't know anything about them, I just picked one. The girl I picked ended up being a pretty boring and non-existent roommate because she was either sleeping or she was never there. But I would soon discover that the girl I didn't choose lived down the hall from me, and we both were interested in applying for the design program.

Over the course of that year, we became very good friends, and we helped each other with design projects along the way. We eventually became roommates during our latter college years, and we even started our very first (officially registered) design business together while still in school. We learned a lot about design together, and we shared some memorable (and laughable) client experiences, and we were able to bounce ideas off one another and grow together as designers. To this day, we are still very close friends, and the bond that we shared through design still remains.

As you begin your journey, you should make friends with other graphic designers. Not just because designers are cool people — although we are — but your graphic designer friends will share a common interest with you. They will understand the journey you are going through because they are going — or have gone — through it, too. They will give you helpful feedback on your work, help you with your projects, and even teach you new skills and techniques.

Another great benefit to finding others who enjoy design just as much as you do is that they can speak your language. Yes, graphic designers do share inside jokes about Pantone colors, complain about font compatibility, and even get excited about the newest Bootstrap update. Your non-designer friends just won't get it — and they may not even care — so surround yourself with other like-minded people who are just as excited about design as you are.

Also, consider joining a design-related club at school, or a social media group, meet-up or association. These groups can provide valuable resources and connections that you may not have gained on your own. They are also great ways to bounce ideas off of others, receive constructive criticism, gain diverse design experiences, and make new friends.

So remember to keep your design super friends close — you will need them!

24. Unplug

Put your hands up, and step away from your computer!

Design overload: when you work on something for so long — editing countless photos, writing endless lines of code, or formatting 300 pages of text — that your brain is literally on the verge of turning into mush. All designers will occasionally suffer from it. After all, graphic designers work hard. We pound away on our computers for countless hours, we warm many a chair, and our eyes see every font, color and overused stock photo known to man. We are responsible for building brands and making peoples' visions come to life. Sometimes we just need to "get it done", and that's understandable. But seriously. Take a break!

UNPLUG

WHEW!

As you begin working, you will discover that saying "yes" to others' demands (like making yet another revision or presenting your concept for the fourth time) becomes frequent, and you might slowly begin to neglect yourself. It's also easy to start thinking that sitting in front of a computer for 18 hours a day is normal. In our world, it might be. To others, it might be a little weird. You have to learn when it's time to give it a rest.

Get away from the screen, and give your eyes and brain a chance to recoup. Thinking creatively or technically is challenging, and it takes a lot of brainpower that can potentially become draining to your mind and body if overdone. If you're in a situation where you're working on someone else's time, there are simple things you can do like taking some time throughout the workday to grab a bite to eat, occasionally stand up, walk around or stretch.

If you aren't constrained by a work or school environment, then you can take breaks like going outside to enjoy nature, watching TV, exercising, talking on the phone, etc. It's even important to take vacations, whether big or small…any type of break to get away from your computer and reset your mind. Whatever the situation, take the time you need to unplug and give yourself the rest that you need to tackle each day at your best. Perhaps you already have a healthy level of restraint and a balanced work/play lifestyle, but if you're like me, force yourself to take a short — or long — break so that your mind can be rejuvenated.

25. Have fun — it's design!

Graphic design is one of the coolest professions on Earth. So because of that, you can't forget to have fun doing it! Work on things that inspire you and excite you. It's really easy to get bogged down with the stresses of working as a graphic designer — multiple projects, refining entire visual brands, editing code, multiple logo revisions, managing an unrealistic deadline, or learning a new skill. And in the midst of the design chaos, it's normal to feel a little burnt out over long periods of time. But don't let those busy moments make you forget why you pursued design in the first place.

AWESOME DESIGN

The great thing about design is that you can reinvent, reinvigorate or re-purpose yourself at any time. In fact, every day is a chance to shine and show your creativity. If you get tired of designing for one industry, try another. If you get bored with print design, dive into interactive design. If you feel like you're stuck designing in the same style, learn new design styles and new ways of thinking about design. You can control what you want your graphic design career to look like.

I have fun as a designer because most of the time, it doesn't feel like work. It's just something that I enjoy. I'm not confined to just working in an office cubicle, but I can work from a laptop on a beach or in the comforts of my own home. I get to work with other designers and meet cool people. I have the unique opportunity to inspire, influence and make big decisions. So although what I do sometimes requires spending hours behind the computer screen, drinking multiple cups of coffee in one sitting or staying up all night, I appreciate and love what I do. And when you love what you do, you're more likely to have fun doing it!

Make sure you have fun during your journey as a graphic designer, and find enjoyment in the projects that you create. Find ways to make your work enjoyable. There are too many opportunities out there to be bored or unsatisfied with your work. Make an effort to discover what aspects of graphic design you like, what drives you, and what you don't mind working on in the middle of the night. When you discover the parts of graphic design you really enjoy, take it and run with it! Your design career is only what you make it.

FOOTNOTES:

1. The Creative Group. *Salary Barista: Your Source for Creative Industry Salary Information.* 2014. PDF file.

Conclusion

I hope after reading this book, you are more excited about your pursuit of graphic design! But while this book has come to an end, your journey is just beginning! There's so much more that you will discover, learn and accomplish. So, as you start your design journey, remember:

- This book is a guide only. It's not meant to replace or be a substitute for any type of formal education. It's up to you to figure out your own path to learning graphic design.
- To always keep an open mind.
- To work hard.
- To be unique.
- You'll make mistakes, but keep going anyway.
- Design is supposed to be fun. Keep it that way.

Now, get busy designing!

About the Author

I'm Shannel Wheeler — a graphic designer, creative thinker and entrepreneur — and I love design so much, I wrote a book about it!

I've been designing professionally for over 10 years, but creating since I was a little kid. I received my Bachelor of Science degree in Visual Communication Design from The (pronounced "thee") Ohio State University and also a graduate certificate in Interactive Design from The Savannah College of Art and Design (SCAD) Atlanta. I've also gotten a heap of design experience from corporate America and from exploring my own business ventures.

I hope to continue sharing my passion for design in fun ways — through teaching, inspiration and innovative projects. In my spare time, I like to laugh, eat, travel, stay active, watch football, play video games, and make each day of life another day of adventure.

Follow me on Twitter at **@Cre8tiveVenting**, like my Facebook page, **Facebook.com/makeawesomedesign** and don't forget to visit **www.makeawesomedesign.com**

www.ingramcontent.com/pod-product-compliance
Lightning Source LLC
Chambersburg PA
CBHW041303290326
41931CB00032B/10